HORSE POWER

SPARKY'S STEM GUIDE TO

MOTORCYCLES

BY KIRSTY HOLMES

KidHaven
PUBLISHING

Published in 2023 by **KidHaven Publishing,**
an Imprint of Greenhaven Publishing, LLC
29 East 21st Street
New York, NY 10010

Edited by: Emilie Dufresne
Designed by: Danielle Rippengill

Cataloging-in-Publication Data

Names: Holmes, Kirsty.
Title: Sparky's STEM guide to motorcycles / Kirsty Holmes.
Description: New York : KidHaven Publishing, 2023. |
Series: Horse power | Includes glossary and index.
Identifiers: ISBN 9781534540330 (pbk.) | ISBN 9781534540354
(library bound) | ISBN 9781534540347
(6 pack) | ISBN 9781534540361 (ebook)
Subjects: LCSH: Motorcycles--Juvenile literature.
Classification: LCC TL440.15 H635 2023 |
DDC 629.227'5--dc23

Printed in the United States of America

CPSIA compliance Information: Batch #CSKH23: For further information contact Greenhaven Publishing
LLC, New York, New York at 1-844-317-7404.

Please visit our website, www.greenhavenpublishing.com. For a free
color catalog of all our high-quality books, call toll free 1-844-317-7404
or fax 1-844-317-7405.

IMAGE CREDITS

All images are courtesy of Shutterstock.com, unless otherwise specified. With thanks to Getty Images, Thinkstock Photo and iStockphoto. Cover – NotionPic,
A–R–T, logika600, BiterBig, Marharyta Pavliuk, SugarDesign. Sparky – NotionPic, Marharyta Pavliuk. Peggy – NotionPic. Grid – BiterBig. Construction School
– Mascha Tace. 2 – . 5 – Mascha Tace. 6 – Ivengo. 7 – MuchMania. 8 – Ivengo. 10 – Flat vectors. 11 – Dzianis_Rakhuba. 12 – KittyVector. 12 & 13 – Ivengo,
MuchMania, 13 – Igogosha. 16 – Alex Leo, Shirstok. 17 – Ivengo. 18 & 19 – MuchMania, KittyVector. 20 – Mascha Tace. 21 – ArtMalivanov, DRogatnev.
22 – Alexandr III, VectorsMarket, Meth Mehr. 23 – Mascha Tace, Alexandr Kahovski.

CONTENTS

WORDS THAT LOOK LIKE this CAN BE FOUND IN THE GLOSSARY ON PAGE 24.

WELCOME TO DRIVING SCHOOL!

VROOM! I'm Jeremy Sparkplug, world-famous motorcycle racer. You can call me Sparky. You must be the new recruits. Welcome to the Horses for Courses School of Motoring!

Here you will be learning about some of the fastest – and coolest – **vehicles** on two wheels: motorcycles! Pay attention, because if you pass your driving test, you'll earn your Golden Horseshoe.

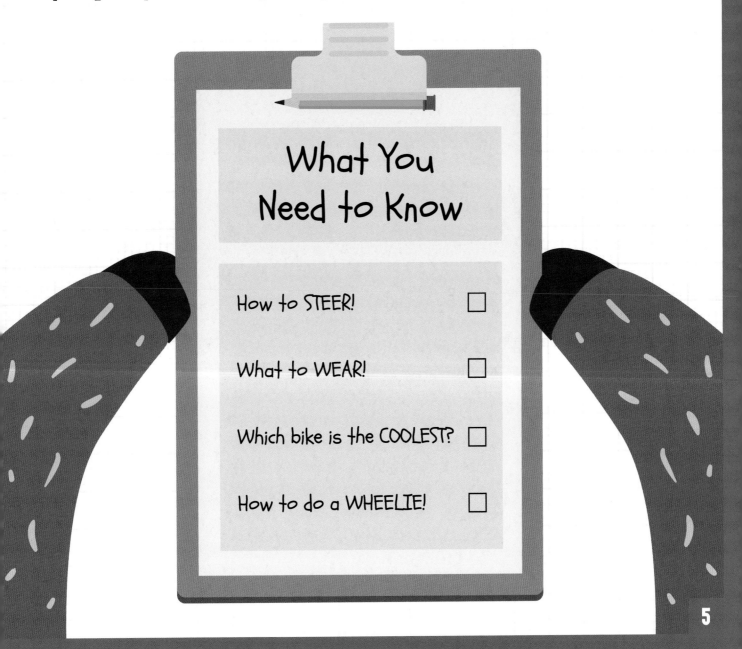

What You Need to Know

How to STEER! ☐

What to WEAR! ☐

Which bike is the COOLEST? ☐

How to do a WHEELIE! ☐

LESSON 1: WHAT IS A MOTORCYCLE?

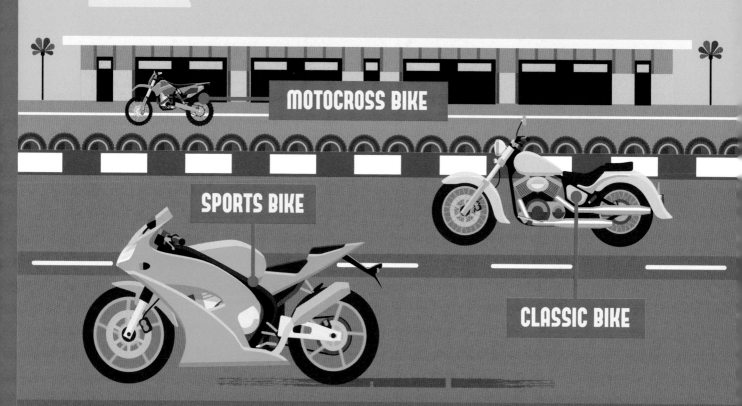

MOTOCROSS BIKE

SPORTS BIKE

CLASSIC BIKE

A motorcycle is a vehicle that usually has two wheels, a seat for the driver (and sometimes a passenger), and an engine. Motorcycles are mostly for getting one or two people from one place to another.

7

PARTS OF A MOTORCYCLE

SUSPENSION

This helps the motorcycle bounce on the road, making the ride more comfortable.

FRONT FORK

This holds the front wheel in place, and allows the rider to steer.

ENGINE

The engine provides the power for the motorcycle.

BRAKES

Brakes stop the motorcycle.

WHEELS

Wheels are made of metal, and have tires that are usually made of **rubber**.

In a car, you are protected from the weather and accidents by the roof and doors. On a motorcycle, your clothing has to do the job of protecting you instead. This special clothing is often called "gear."

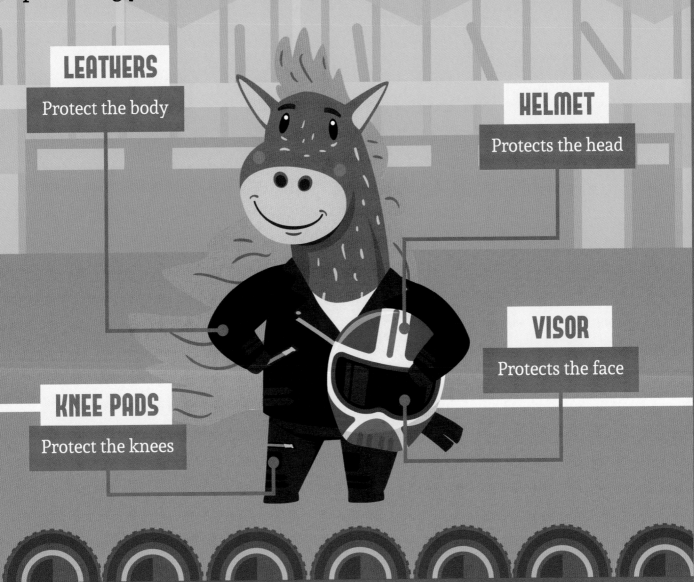

LEATHERS
Protect the body

HELMET
Protects the head

VISOR
Protects the face

KNEE PADS
Protect the knees

LESSON 3: RIDING A MOTORCYCLE

Let's take a look at the **dashboard** to see how to steer and control a motorcycle.

CLUTCH LEVER
This is for selecting and changing **gear**.

SPEEDOMETER
This tells the rider how fast they are going.

TACHOMETER
This helps the rider know when to change gear.

MIRRORS
The rider uses these to see behind them.

BRAKE LEVER
This is for slowing down and stopping.

LIGHT SWITCH
This turns the lights on and off.

HANDLEBARS
These steer the motorcycle.

THROTTLE
Twisting this handgrip controls the speed of the motorcycle.

Some motorcycles have only one seat, but others have a second seat for passengers. This second seat is sometimes called the pillion seat. Passengers on a bike are "riding pillion."

LESSON 4:
TYPES OF MOTORCYCLES

There are lots of different types of motorcycles.
Let's look at some of the more popular ones.

SCOOTERS

Scooters have a platform for the rider's feet.

TOURING BIKES

These are sturdy and comfortable for riding long distances.

SPORTS BIKES

These are built for speed and power. They are **designed** for roads and racing tracks.

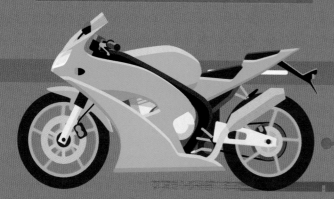

CHOPPERS

These **custom-built** motorcycles are designed for style, not speed.

OFF-ROAD BIKES

These are built for tracks, sand, mud, snow, and racing off the roads.

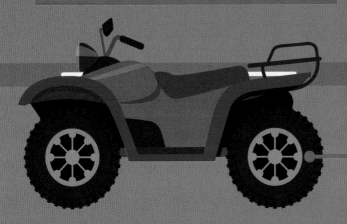

QUAD BIKES

These have four wheels.

STEERING!

You might think steering a motorbike is just like steering your bike in the park. However, there is a little more to it than that...

STEER IN THE DIRECTION YOU WANT TO GO...

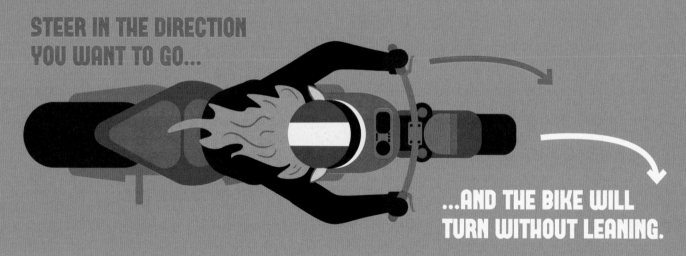

...AND THE BIKE WILL TURN WITHOUT LEANING.

SLOW SPEEDS

To turn right at slow speeds, you push the left handlebar forward and pull the right one towards you.

FAST SPEEDS

At fast speeds, instead of pushing the left handlebar, you slightly push the right one. The bike leans the opposite way, and **arcs** around the turn. This is called countersteering.

STEER

Steer in the opposite direction, just for a moment...

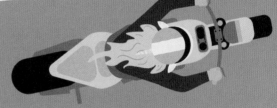

TURN

...and the bike will lean into the turn.

WHEELIES!

OK, class. While Sparky is distracted polishing his bike, I'm going to teach you something really, really cool. This is how to do a wheelie...

STEP ONE

Start slowly, at around 10 miles (16 km) per hour.

STEP TWO

Hit the throttle and speed up – hard!

STEP THREE

Lean back and pull the front wheel up... Wheelie!

It takes a lot of practice to do the perfect wheelie – so when you're older, and you've passed all your tests, I'll give you another lesson!

MEGA MOTORCYCLE

THE REGIO DESIGN XXL CHOPPER

Fabio Reggiani's custom-built chopper is one of the world's biggest motorcycles. It is over 16 feet (5 m) tall, almost 33 feet (10 m) long, and weighs about 8,820 pounds (4,000 kg)!

THE TIRES ARE 6.5 FEET (2 M) ACROSS!

DRIVING TEST

Bikers, it's time to earn your Golden Horseshoe. Safely make your way to the test center... I said safely! Who taught you to do a wheelie like that... and can they teach me? (Check your answers on page 21!)

Questions

1. What does the suspension do?

2. What does a visor protect?

3. What is "riding pillion"?

4. When countersteering, which handlebar should you push first if you want to go right?

5. How tall is the Regio Design XXL Chopper?

Did you get them all right?

Of course you did – here is your Golden Horseshoe. You are now officially in the Cool Bikers Club, just like Peggy and me!

RAMP TO RAMP

Motorcycles are great for getting around, having fun on the track, and looking cool. But in our expert hooves, they are also great for WILD, CRAZY STUNTS!

STEP ONE
Get some buses...

STEP TWO
Ramp it up...

STEP THREE
Start your engines...

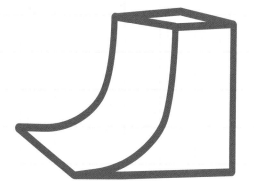

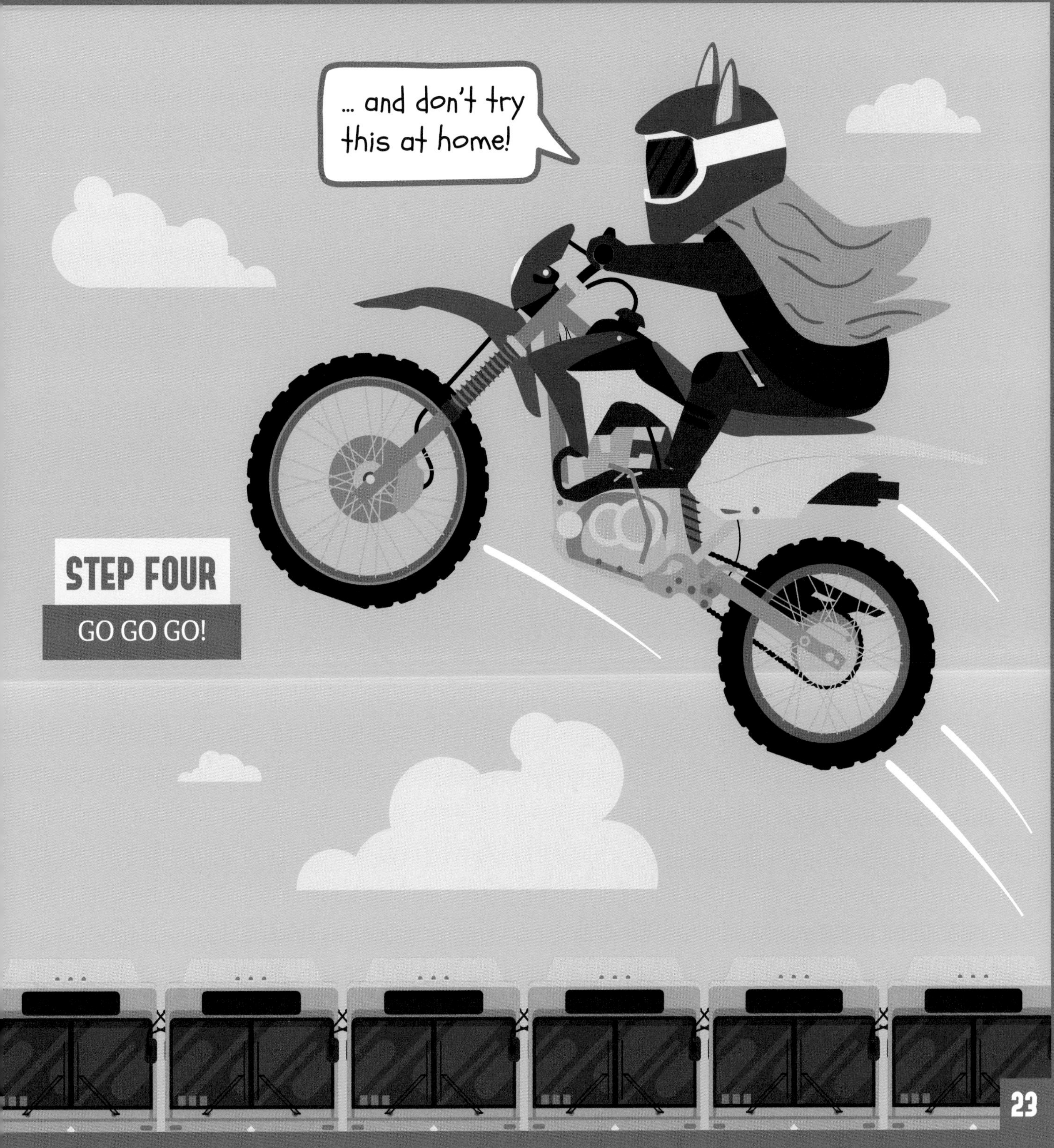

STEP FOUR

GO GO GO!

GLOSSARY

ARCS travels on a curved line or path

CUSTOM-BUILT built specially for one person, exactly how they want it

DASHBOARD the area facing the driver of a vehicle, which contains the controls for driving

DESIGNED specially made for a specific purpose

GEAR a part of a machine that moves other parts

RUBBER a bouncy material made from tropical plants

VEHICLES machines used for carrying or transporting things or people

INDEX